WHAT
THE
BODY
TOLD

WHAT
THE
BODY
TOLD

Rafael Campo

DUKE UNIVERSITY PRESS | DURHAM & LONDON 1996

"Song Before Dying," "DNA, or, The Legend of My
Grandfather," and "The Doctor" have appeared in
The Kenyon Review.
"My Childhood in Another Part of the World" has appeared
in *The American Voice.*
"*El Día de los Muertos*," "An Obsession with Curlers" and
portions of "Ten Patients, and Another" have appeared in
The Threepenny Review.
Other portions of "Ten Patients, and Another" have
appeared in *Parnassus: Poetry in Review.*
"My Voice" has appeared in *The Nation.*
"I Become Charlotte" has appeared in *Harvard Magazine.*
"Confession," "So in Love," "What We All Want," and
"Lost in the Hospital" have appeared in *Gulf Coast.*
"The Battle Hymn of the Republic" has appeared in
Ploughshares and was selected to be reprinted in *Best
American Poetry 1995.*
"In English That Is Spanish," "The 10,000th AIDS
Death in San Francisco," "Madrid," and "The Cuban
Sky" have appeared in *Prairie Schooner.*
"Defining Us" and "Asylum" have appeared in *Poetry
Ireland Review.*
"Prescription" and "Before Safe Sex" have appeared
in *ZYZZYVA.*
"For You All Beauty" has appeared in *Gents, Badboys, and
Barbarians,* an anthology of new gay male poets.
"The Passive Voice" has appeared in *Badboys,* an
anthology of erotic gay male poetry.
© 1996 Duke University Press   All rights reserved
Third printing, 2004
Printed in the United States of America on
acid-free paper ∞   Typeset in Galliard
Library of Congress Cataloging-in-Publication Data
appear on the last printed page of this book.

For Mary,
Marilyn,
and dearest Eve—

Love fairies,
queer angels in
poetry

Heaven—airily
descend,
and give to me

What's scary
once again:
the belief

That I can write
and love J.A. all night,

Telling what is true.
This book is for you.

CONTENTS

I Defining Us

II Canciones de la Vida

III For You All Beauty

IV Canciones de la Muerte

V What the Body Told

WHAT
THE
BODY
TOLD

I

DEFINING

US

So in Love

It's not so hard to deviate.
I saw him once. He sat and ate
A fruit that looked delicious, sweet,

So natural. He looked at me.
I think he looked up lovingly.
I think he thought of knocking me

Upside the head. I saw him, once,
A distant smile. I wondered when.
I wondered when. I saw the fence

I still believe invisibly
Might fence me out; there, distantly,
I saw embraces incomplete,

How trees grow naturally in fields
Thick, healthful fruits. His skin, like steel.
His mouth, what I constantly feel

At my mouth, murmuring these words.
It's not so hard to love. I heard
Him crash through trees, through fields. I learned.

Route 17

Just after I had landed my first job—
they needed busboys at the Mexican
chain restaurant that opened where Lake crossed
Route 17, an intersection known
in town for being dangerous—we met.
Among my new responsibilities
was polishing the silverware, he said
while pointing a dull butter knife at me.
He plunged it in a pitcher full of seltzer,
and for a moment it was diamond-jeweled
in carbonation, like some priceless dagger
belonging to a king.
                              I wasn't fooled.
His muscle shirts and dancing skills combined
suggested his were pleasures of a sort
not more sophisticated, but *sublime*—
a word I memorized expressly for
the SAT's. I planned to go away
to college—Massachusetts, maybe Maine,
which seemed as far away from Jersey as anyplace
could be. My parents didn't have the means
to pay the huge tuitions, so I had
to work. The friends I made, including Al,
agreed: what I needed to get ahead
was words.
                    He also managed a motel
for extra cash. He teased the waitresses;
the constant flirting reassured me. One
named Abby—poverty had made her wise,
at least to me, enamored of the green
tattoo inside her arm—suspected it.
Her ex and her best friend together formed
a band (they called themselves The Opiates)
which played at local clubs and senior proms
until they shocked her with the truth. "All queers
are obvious to me," she told me as

I kissed her tiny freckled breasts, unsure
of my performance.
                         Al was somewhere else
The night I got so drunk I could have done
whatever I imagined he might want
me to. They poured me Cuba Libres, rum
so sweet it made me want to stay, not quit
and go to college. Abby whispered in
my ear, her lips as thick as fingers: "Stay
with me." I wondered why he looked so thin.
I'd noticed how his clothes were ruffled by
the wind as he crossed 17 to get
his car; they seemed a size too big. Unclear
on who I was, I wanted him. "Forget
him, look at me," gnawed Abby on my ear.
I did.
           Just three months later, Al was dead.
It was the spring of 1983,
before the shuttle with astronauts
exploded. When I took the SAT's
I thought of him, the night we saw that wreck
on 17. Six drunken teenagers
from town had crashed head-on into a truck.
Before the ambulance arrived, I heard
Al calling to them, darting underneath
the traffic light, the whole world stopped around
him. Trying crumpled doors, the oily heat
of radiator steam released, he found
their broken bodies first.
                                  On 17,
he must have been infected; most rest stops
along the highway to New York were scenes
for cruising. Bodies pressed to bodies, cops
with flashlights peering into cars—today
it seems less glamorous to me. Back then,
the new disease that ravaged Al—("I'm gay,"
he finally confessed, above the din
of Happy Hour in the mirrored bar

as I was finishing my shift. "You need
a ride somewhere?" I hurried to my car . . .)—
seemed so momentous, meaningful as blood.
I wished I had been brave enough, for him;
today, the words I learn seem guarded, grim.

The Crying Game

Lost hopelessly, the terrorist begins
To know remorse. He lights a cigarette;
The glow illuminates his face. The woods
Are deep, and he is searching for the part
Of his unlikely friend he loved the most.
His own erection startled him. It felt
So good, the two of them alone beneath
A sky of anonymity, the sigh
Of some potential danger lurking there
Beneath their canopy of dying leaves.
The woods grow deeper, like his eyes grew deep
The more he stared at him. The terrorist
Begins to know remorse; he touches it
Beneath the moon, as if to find the part
Of him that's lost so hopelessly it might
Be gone forever. Trying not to fall
In love, he meets a sorceress who cuts
His hair. She changes his identity.
She sucks his cock, pretending to be weak.
It feels so good. Remembering his friend,
He lights a cigarette and sighs. He can't
Recall what he was searching for, except
He knows it had to do with love. He sucks
Until the fire at the tip begins
To burn his lips. The woods are deep, and in
The sorceress he finds a mystery.
He enters her as one might enter woods
To look for one's lost friend. Inside her chest,
He finds her heart, but he mistakes it for
The moon; between her legs, he finds a thick
Erection pointing out his face, the sky
Of anonymity, the way toward freedom.
The terrorist begins to know remorse.

Asylum

Demented underneath the moon, I watch
The street conduct electric sparks tonight,
These cars, their headlights, energy in flight—

Skyscrapers precarious as men in heels.
This night, it seems more glamorous than real.
Demented underneath the moon, around

Another corner, ten men beat the pan
Of shiny, pooling blood another man
Has made for them, his whole life's work: these men

Identified another queer. The moon,
Demented underneath the fleeting stars,
Demented, shining on the speeding cars,

Dissolves upon my tongue. It tastes like force.
It tastes like blood, saliva, teeth. I'd curse,
But I'm demented. Underneath the moon,

The moonlight makes perfection out of me.
The men are beating on their drum. Their drums
Are poverty and ignorance, so painfully

Made lucid. Once, I really saw the moon.
It hurt. And underneath it all the world
Was busy, furious, bent to the loom.

The Passive Voice

Imagine why a man likes being fucked.
Imagine how my cock likes being sucked.
Imagine making love to me, my friend.

In English class, my teacher told us not
To use the passive voice; "It's weak," he said.
There was an older man who sometimes knocked

At my back door; I'd think of him in bed
And wonder if he'd like to make it break.
Imagine making love to him, my friend,

Until your mother finds your door unlocked.
Imagine what it's like slowly to bend
Beneath another man's gigantic cock—

The pleasures of the asshole aren't discerned
By many English teachers (mine was like
The handsome man I'd like to love instead)—

Imagine telling him. Of course, he's shocked,
But after several weeks a note he sends:
"Imagine why a man likes being fucked,"

It says, and inexplicably so sad,
"Imagine how my cock likes being sucked."
In high school, no one seems to understand

This kind of love. It could be called dumb luck
Or disappointment, what happened in his bed;
Imagining why men like being fucked,

After his gentle, upright cock, I spent
The night in tears while in his arms I rocked.
Imagine making love to me, my friend.
Imagine why a man likes being fucked.

Before Safe Sex

Once I read poems by Sappho so discreetly
I thought that no one even noticed me.
Then I found an unknown fragment—really,
Stripped from inside a mummy's thigh. "Kiss me,"
It began, and that was all. I began
To write, kissing a man so my copy
Would be right, trembling pen in my hand,
So perfect did I want. But something stopped me—
I really loved this man, where my lips
Kept beginning and beginning, where my thigh
Kept being found—but when I say his hips,
My cock—Sappho my strength!—my tongue is tied
In an excruciating knot. I want
Honesty, same as your kiss, so it haunts.

The Battle Hymn of the Republic

Defending you, my country, hurts
My eyes. I see the drums, the glory,
The marching through the gory,
Unthinkable mud of soldiers' guts

And opened hearts: I want to serve.
I join the military,
Somehow knowing that I'll never marry.
The barracks' silence as I shave

Is secretive and full of cocks.
I think to myself, *What if I'm a queer,*
What if too many years
Go by and then my brain unlocks —

The days seem uniformed,
Crisp salutes in all the trees;
A sandstorm buries the casualties
Of a war. *What if I were born*

This way, I think to myself,
What if I were dead,
An enemy bullet in my head?
I see the oil burning in the Gulf,

Which hurts my eyes. My sergeant cries.
Now he's a real man —
I sucked his cock behind a van
In the Presidio, beneath a sky

So full of orange clouds
I thought I was in love.
I think to myself, *What have*
I become? I lose myself in the crowds

Of the Castro, the months go by
And suddenly they want to lift the ban.
I don't think they can.
I still want to die

My death of honor, I want to die
Defending values I don't understand;
The men I see walking hand in hand
Bring this love song to my mind.

Defining Us

No knowledge is more powerful
Than knowing love, than knowing how
To love despite a world so full

Of the intent to hate. I know
Of others who are like me now.
I've seen us on *Arsenio*;

I've seen us march on Washington,
The love I felt so deep I feared
It was a dream. But one in ten

Of us, supposedly, got stunned
In utero with something queer,
A sort of poison laser gun

(A hormone gone berserk, some say,
While others tout a faulty gene).
All that I know is this: I'm gay,

And knowledge is less powerful
Than love, and that whatever dream
I have, in him it is fulfilled.

I Become Charlotte

With Massachusetts rotaries ahead
Our only obstacles besides ourselves,
We drive to Beverly for Charlotte. Men
From Saugus on their way to Endicott
Roar by in open jeeps. We have maps, those
Mysterious directions Charlotte gave;
The expectation of arriving safe
Is Kathy's Volvo station wagon. Light,
The miles, more minutes fill the car. We laugh
At missing exits: what would Charlotte think?
Our Charlotte is a poet. Innocent,
And gay. She even has a decent job.
She's teaching adolescents from Japan
An English as a Foreign Language course.
She handles Hiroshima, disciplines
The boys who gather seaweed on the beach
Past dark, and when her day is over, when
She sits, her antique desk is sentences
Erupting through her typewriter. She writes
Of Beverly, dead Hiroshima, men
From Saugus raping girls at Endicott,
And how she hates her job. Her lover Joan
Is living with a man in Martinique.
Apparently, they've bought a beachside bar.
I know she writes a poem for her, and hears
How English has a foreign language sound.
And as the highway's given over to
More frequent clapboard houses, traffic lights,
White cats that slink across the street, I guess
We're almost there. I think what Charlotte thinks.

My Feminine Side

to Robyn Selman

Not introspective. Not the girl who waits
With timid, flitting eyelashes for him
While sitting in a chair that looks away
From windows toward the center of her room—

The woman I have been is less the art
Of staring at herself, is more her need
Of opening out loud her deepest hurt,
Daring to hoist her skirt up sluttishly

Above her head. But she can't hide from me.
She knows that I have seen her private parts,
And understand how being entered means
You're never safe at midnight crossing parks

To get to that illuminated portal
Where, hopefully, you'll say you're nearly home.
The woman I have been is not immortal,
Nor free. She hates the way I use her name,

And that I speak for her enrages us.
You see, we share the same experience.
Her mind, my body are contiguous
And overlapping. When we try to dance,

The mirror in between us makes it weird:
I crush her toes beneath my clumsy feet,
She looks at me as if she knew the word
That I am looking for: *palimpsest, greed,*

Avuncular—so why won't she speak? Why
Am I so criminal to her? I guess
The jeans I wear she finds offensive, my
Queer haircut not too flattering, my shoes

Embarrassingly out-of-date. If I
Could tell her how I really felt, entire
Worlds melting in my throat, she'd never die.
We'd bend together close, intent at our lyre.

Once There Was Great Love

for M.H. and K.L.
March 14, 1993

Once, I saw women—two of them, or groups of
Three or four—all dancing a kind of danceless,
Woebegone, and incomprehensibly love-
Crazed dance. Gone speechless

Watching, I turned to poetry. I floundered.
Words for love escaped from my tongue, and something
Deep inside kept telling this lie: *you'll find her,*
And then your singing

Will in a boundless moment be regarded
Beautiful. The pain of it all was that I
Knew those women lounging about my garden
Were made of tears, cries

Lesbians made through distant separations,
Lips to breasts through angry ex-husbands' thunder,
Making love and wielding their power. Nations
Like mine may wonder

Why it is women who possess such strengths, not
Men. Because—we hate to admit it—men are
Given to a gaze at the world so bloodshot
It causes cancer.

Women survivors, paired with one another,
Mate for life most times; in a city all know,
Registering couples ("domestic partners")
Find happiness. So

Don't cry for them. Instead, allow them storefront
Restaurants, alive in the dim, romantic
Candlelight; that's love in their eyes. They're decent
People, though some think

Singing of them, the way I do, is sinful.
How can it be so? With her hands, my mother
Combed the universe for her box of seashells,
Perfumes, dried flowers—

Feminine things she only touched in private.
Thinking of her face in the mirror's silver,
All the love of women inside her magnet-
Heart, for her, in her—

That's how I know. She loved each day completely,
Womanly, serene as the motion sunlight
Makes across a tablecloth's white expanse. She
Taught me to songwrite:

Once there was great love. Women made it. Then, as
Time began, the women stayed free, like spirits.
Everything is yours in her arms. The years passed;
Love never ended.

II

CANCIONES

DE LA

VIDA

CANCIÓN DE LAS MUJERES

for Eve Kosofsky Sedgwick

I. Some Uses for the Moon

The moon provides comparison: behold,
A woman staring in her mirror. Light
Is how the moon accompanies the night,
And helps to ease the loneliness. (I'm told
The moon is why a woman menstruates.)
The moon could be, if only we could reach
So high, the perfect soup that cures our needs.
In Cuba, moonlight on the sea has weight—
One ounce—against which fortunes can be measured.
The moon's an oddity, a dried-out bone;
The moon's my palace, and a peasant's home.
The moon, a satin pillow filled with feathers . . .
The moon provides this starting place for myth,
And as we're wandering the beach, it's sand
On which is made a princess from a man:
The moon is climbing slowly from the mist.

II. My Mother's Closet

The belts behind the door, a waterfall.
The pumps lined up, small soldiers at attention;
The hats, and scarves too numerous to mention.
I wandered, wishing I could wear it all—
Except my mom was tall and thin, while I
Was built more like a man. The dry-cleaned silk
Of unborn dresses, waiting for the milk
Of her white skin beneath them: brought to life,
The red one was a wound that never healed;
The blue one was a river that might drown
Us both; the gold lamé was like a cloud
Of fairy dust. Beside those shoes, I'd kneel
As though I'd found a secret pool in which
To bathe. I'd pray for strength and privacy,
For us. I'd cleanse myself, until I'd see
My face was hers, beyond the mirror's reach.

III. Fat

She read in *Cosmopolitan* last week
That men just aren't interested in
A woman's mind, the music nestled in
Her voice, or anything besides how sleek
Her dress is, spread across her thighs. She learns
To hide her panty lines, place cucumbers
Upon her eyes to smooth the wrinkles there,
To exercise until her muscles burn:
It's hard for her to see her cellulite
Herself since where it's worst—behind the thigh—
Is nowhere land. She's always known that guys
Hate fat. And every time she takes a bite
Of something that tastes good to her, she knows
She's being punished for some lack of will.
She can't eat cake until she's had her fill;
With exercise, she prays her breasts will grow.

IV. Revulsion

I think her name was Carly—no, Charlene.
So fucking beautiful, the way she laughed,
A hardness in her face that seemed so soft.
She picked up Jerry real quick—I mean,
Without his knowing it—they dated three,
Four months. He kissed her in the parking lot
One night in front of all our friends. We thought
She was a woman, too. Eventually,
He wanted more than just a kiss; she played
Miss frightened innocent until he forced
His hand inside her dress. Her bloody face
Was in the local newspapers next day,
Beneath the one-inch headline MALE PROSTITUTE
FOUND DEAD. I recognized her, sure I did,
But I would say she got what she deserved—
I mean, she was a guy, a fucking fruit.

V. Her Final Show

She said it was a better way to die
Than most; she seemed relieved, almost at peace,
The stench of her infected Kaposi's
Made bearable by the Opium applied
So daintily behind her ears: "I know
It costs a lot, but dear, I'm nearly gone."
Her shade of eyeshadow was emerald green;
She clutched her favorite stones. Her final show
She'd worn them all, sixteen necklaces of pearls,
Ten strings of beads. She said they gave her hope.
Together, heavy as a gallow's rope,
The gifts of drag queens dead of AIDS. "Those girls,
They gave me so much strength," she whispered as
I turned the morphine up. She hid her leg
Beneath smoothed sheets. I straightened her red wig
Before pronouncing her to no applause.

VI. Woman Driver

The sun is pouring through the car—watch out,
Since I'm a maniac! I drive to kill.
My sunglasses project an air of skill,
But do not be deceived. So turn and shout,
"You stupid bitch! You whore! You stupid cunt!"
I won't be listening. I'm trapped behind
This glass the sun is pouring through; my mind
Is elsewhere, hidden from all view. I won't
Let anyone hurt me again: I drive
To kill. I've got my license and the vote,
Swept up my mother's shattered gravy boat,
And told the man I love he should behave
Before he slugged me in the face. That's why
I wear these sunglasses—to hide the bruise.
You glimpse me through the glass, you stupid brutes,
Before you honk your horns. I drive and drive.

VII. *Las Mujeres*

They talk until the night is dark like jungles,
Until they deep like poetry and dreams,
Until the stars is jewelry ain't no crime
For them to wear, the talking like the muscles
No woman is supposed to have, and shit
The women in my crazy neighborhood
I know that some of them, you know, don't bleed,
More Tarzan than me-Jane, they way they sit,
The city close on them as a date with Tom Cruz,
And that's the way it should be spelt down here,
Down here where it's almost Cuba, them queers
With them fine women talking like it's ours,
Like anything belongs to us and don't
They know they lucky no one kills them, shit
I almost died myself just watching it,
Them talking, fags with dreams big as their hands.

VIII. Silence of the Lambs

It's dangerous to think this way: I saw
A movie yesterday in which a man
Who wants to be a woman drives a van
To parking lots and captures one—she's drawn
To him because he's helpless and he needs
To move his couch—and then he starves her at
The bottom of a well. He chooses fat
Girls since the motive for his awful deeds
Is that their skin is the material
He uses in the dress he's sewing for
Himself—a gown of women's skin. I'm sure
They don't mean me, I think—I hear her call
To him from deep inside, she's suffering,
Afraid, and I identify with her,
Except I want to shed my skin, then turn
To everything that isn't butterflies.

IX. Divine

The movies weren't big enough for you.
Offensive, feminine, gigantic, wild—
"The most beautiful woman in the world"
You called yourself, while shattering taboos
Celebrities in Hollywood long feared.
The movies weren't mad enough for you,
Their filth was still too clean. Your true debut
In *Pink Flamingos* branded you a queer:
Divinity was eating shit, a man
In drag both glamorous and in bad taste.
The movies weren't made enough in haste
For you, three hundred pounds in so much pain
Of those high heels. Your death was overdue,
You might have said, intolerant of all
That's not outrageous—older, growing ill,
The movies not in time enough for you.

X. Men Get the Shaft

It's true—that men get shafted all the time.
Who really wants the power to destroy
The world? And think of all the little boys
Who learn to squelch their tears before the tombs
Of their beloved pets! It's true—men get
The shaft. In college, they're the ones the prof
Will always call upon to give the proof;
It doesn't even matter where they sit,
In front or back. It's true, all right. Recall
The many catalogues for women's clothes;
For men there's few. (The manly mind is closed
To fashion—looking good means at some mall
You lean against a wall and leer.) It's true
Men get the shaft, and literally, too.
Behind their zippers, faintly outlined, you
Can sometimes make it out, that inch or two.

XI. An Obsession with Curlers

My mother's looked like an ingenious
Device to read another person's mind
Or see if we were coming from behind,
Or to project her thoughts on all of us.
They made the family afraid of her.
What's more, they seemed to have the side effects
Of temporary deafness (while she waxed
Her eyebrows), and of amplifying hair.
When she'd arrange them in their box to heat
Them up—when they were warm, a light would blink—
They looked like they were dials that could shrink
The dog if properly employed. I'd hate
It when she put them all away. It meant
That she was done, and would be going out
That night. I tried to read her mind; I'd pout
(And that was how she knew) before she went.

XII. Fear of Elevators

It's not exactly claustrophobia.
I just can't help it—noticing the man
Who's getting on the next floor down. I can't
Help noticing the tiny scar he's got
Beneath his chin, or that he doesn't carry
Some packages to say he's shopping here.
He looks suspicious, dark. I look for where
The built-in phone is, praying for the lobby—
Security, the women shoppers, guards—
But this descent is too controlled, too slow,
Resisting gravity's pull as we go
Down, lower, lower, never skipping floors:
This man is raping me by now, I feel
His knife-point pressing just beneath my chin,
The slightly oily texture of his skin—
I weigh a little less as I'm forced to kneel.

XIII. Miss Key West, 1990

The competition's keen: ten women, all
Among the most accomplished in the state.
The crowd is elegant, fifty-bucks-a-plate.
We wait. The women's names are sensual,
Implying appetites and certain tastes,
Meringues and chocolates, and sweet champagne.
I'm just a tourist here—I only came
Because I'm curious. But when a toast
Is raised to the performers by a man
In drag, I feel glamorous, that I
Belong beneath some spotlight too, divine,
The baubles dripping from my ears, so tan
I'm drenched in gold, I'm what you see
When light is passing through a bottle of
Perfume, or when you're powerlessly in love:
I'm Cuba's tears, I'm fashion magazines.

XIV. Imagining Drag

I think that illness is a form of drag:
The body dresses in the gossamer
Of death, as thin as fog upon a moor,
The cemetery's moon a kind of drug
That makes forgetting possible. I think
That writing poetry is just as queer:
Adorning language with a rhyme as clear
As diamonds dangled from the ear. The link
Is not as tenuous as it might seem.
To die, to write in artificial meter,
To wear beneath a suit a silken girdle—
Each has everything to do with dreams,
Their loss and their attainment equally
Ungainly, equally too fanciful.
Perimeters are what the fingers feel,
Where what the eyes can touch is all we see.

XV. The Fat Lady Sings

It's impossible to change your gender;
People change their sex through surgical pro-
Cedures though. Cross-dressing means you're into
Opposites in terms of clothes, but gender
Really isn't what's at stake: illusion,
And empowerment that comes from breaking
Rules, is what's behind the risk-taking.
Sexuality must be excluded
From discussion of these gender issues,
Insofar as object choice (of same-sex,
Hetero, the self, or other agents
Of the act of sex *per se*) is found to
Vary through a spectrum in both men and
Women, biological or not. In
Fact, "identity" is merely fiction—
Think of it—we're more than men or women.

XVI. The Last Great Empress of the Dark

I specialize in reading palms. A witch,
A fortune-teller, psychic, sorceress.
A hooker in a thirty-dollar dress?
I know where you can find her, sell your watch
For cash to pay for drugs, or where the clue
That solves the murder can be found. I see
Your future. Tell me all your fantasies,
Or pay me, and I'll guess at what you do.
I also know the past: midwifery,
And women burning at the stake. Back then,
My powers were too threatening for men.
(I majored in medieval history.)
Among my numerous past lives, I've been
Both Joan of Arc and Princess Grace; I saw
That when a nation falls in love, its law
Is to consume its women, one by one.

SONG FOR OUR DAUGHTER

for my sister, Michelle Campo

I. Mother and Daughter

I have one nightmare that I can't elude:
I've read these sonnets to my son. He falls
Asleep. He looks like me. His father calls
From somewhere deep inside the house. I look
At him before I leave. I never get
Downstairs. Instead, I hear a shriek from deep
Inside his room. The hallway is my sleep.
I race to him, my breasts are drenched in sweat,
I somehow reach his door. His crib—I see
A shadow cross the moon—instead of him,
But just as deep inside the crib, a grin
From where a daughter lies. She's terribly
Emaciated, and she speaks in tongues
Except she's not possessed, she's wise. The urge
To mother her, then to abandon her
Is suffocating as it fills my lungs.

II. Elise

I'll name my daughter after you, Elise,
Since naming is what you do best. The heart
You named with poetry; you named with art
As if it were as obvious as peace
The varied torments of the human soul.
I see you pass beneath, as Hardy might,
A lighted window where a girl sits, slight
And wonderful, to watch the falling snow.
You name her all that's joyous in the night,
You name her sorrows all angelic names.
At the edge of a field, you name the ageless scheme—
It's very quiet—of accumulating white.
You name it bottomless, you name it time
And time again. As Hardy might. Elise,
My daughter, name me too. Give me peace.
Name the white slum that is my heart sublime.

III. Daddy's Little Girl

He has a soft spot for his little girl.
I understand it better now because
I have a daughter of my own. I close
My eyes and think of him. Protective. Small—
I think he must have known it all along.
I think of him at Little League, the stands
Ridiculous with parents needing ends
To justify their means. I felt so strong
When he applauded that I knew I'd be
OK. I knew I was his daughter, son,
And most of all, the only little runt
He'd die defending. Masculinity
Has definition in the feminine.
It's dangerous because the vulnerable—
The grandfather, the boy-daughter, your girl—
Can get to you. My team would never win.

IV. My Mother, Painting Her Nails Red

She brings her out, by tiny tugs and jerks.
I hold her hand. We walk to school. It's cold.
I see my stories freezing as they're told:
My father's smoke, my brother's awful jokes—
My mother, rising to those beautiful
Tall oaks outside her window where she'd stand,
So beautiful, so tall, I'd understand
The mystery of the confessional.
I see my mother in my daughter. All
I know—conspiracies as it begins
To snow—is that my mother's oiled skin
Was infinite as dropping down a well,
And just as soft as whispering. I'd cry
When she'd confess her misery to me;
I couldn't understand. She wasn't free.
The oaks: among them, cardinals would fly.

V. Guy and Doll

I was afraid to hold her, since I broke
My cousin Cheryl's china cup (the tea
Was only water from the tap) when we
Were little kids. We played with dolls, small folk
Who always seemed so sad. I tried to hold
The babies carefully, but Cheryl said
I hurt them frightfully since boys were made
From poisoned kinds of rocks and bones—
And I believed her, since I knew that girls
Got baby dolls and china sets. Besides,
The look of dull, flat terror in her eyes,
I mean the doll's, absorbed me from the world
And made me realize that I was mean.
I'm not afraid to hold her anymore,
I mean my daughter now—although, the door
Is open wide so anyone can see.

VI. My Daughter and Her Best Friend
Writing Poems Upstairs

The ease with which they kiss, and share
Their bodies, decorating them with strings
Of beads and feather earrings; when they sing,
It's bread with milk. They braid each other's hair.
This private literary life is theirs:
The witch before her cauldron casting spells,
The lesbians who on sabbatical
Write steamy romance novels, homemakers
Who keep thick journals for their writers' groups—
A world exists that's not exactly free
Of men (so here I am, downstairs) but needs
Us very little. Realized while cooking soup.
I call them to come eat. They thunder down,
Like something breaking. Giggling, a pause:
I turn to watch them enter, holding hands.
"We're you and Jorge!" Makeup thick as clowns.

VII. The Princess and the Pea

My version of the fable goes like this:
A king who lost his daughter in a plague
Beseeches, in his grief, an ugly hag
To bring her back to life. His tenderness
Is moving to her, so she grants his wish.
She gives him what she calls a poisoned pea,
Instructing him to place it underneath
The mattress where she slept while feverish.
That night, upon returning to the castle,
He pauses when he sees her ghostly face
In the grey smoke rising in the fireplace.
Delirious himself with plague, he swallows
The pea, believing he was swindled. Death
Returns, and in his arms he brings the girl.
He leaves her in the parlor with a pearl
Upon her tongue, to witness his last breath.

VIII. She Says Chivalry Is Dead

My daughter idolizes them. She punched
An older boy in school the other day.
She says he'd told her that her ass looked great;
She says she tried to warn him over lunch
The day before. Some guys are really dumb,
She says. Last week, before she joined the League
Of Women Voters Juniors group, some geek
She says whose invitation to the prom
She'd just declined replied by saying that
A woman never could be President.
Instead of punching him, my daughter bent
His glasses in her fist, then stole his hat.
(She reassures us that she isn't queer.)
She's watching *Thelma and Louise* again,
Instead of going out—her only friends,
She says, we understand. And cheer.

IX. Sonnet for the Portuguese

How do I love thee? Let me count the ways.
I love you for your femininity;
I love you for your masculinity.
I love you most because you're Portuguese
And you escaped your father, loved a man,
And married him with all the poetry
There ever was. I love your poetry
Because my daughter was another man
Until imagination by your hand
Had rescued me. I love *Aurora Leigh.*
And though you really weren't Portuguese
You taught me never, never to withstand
An ugliness disguised as circumstance.
I love the sonnets that you made for love.
I love you, since you made my daughter live.
Let's to our daughters dedicate this dance.

X. Rice and Beans

We're cooking rice and beans. It's women's work.
My mother married, learned the recipe—
Got angry chopping onions, gossiping
And hissing over quickly frying pork.
I try to teach it to my daughter, but
It isn't women's work to her, it's not
A culture anymore; she hasn't got
A grandmother whose Cuban appetite
To serve her husband rice and beans each night,
Dependably for years, was more like starving.
She almost made my mother Cuban, carving
Roasts, serving Spanish *tortas*, taking bites
As if she weren't hungry to this day.
My daughter is a vegetarian,
Or so she claims. I want to feed her beans
To fatten her. I know this single way.

XI. Somewhere in Zambia

And now she wants to change her name. She reads
About South Africa, the Nubians,
The Peace Corps, AIDS. She came from Zambia;
That's all we knew, besides what shots she'd need
To enter the United States. We thought,
As parents almost always will, that we
Were saving her from tragic destiny—
Forgetting all the while, as children taught
Their parents' errors almost always will,
That she was saving us. Identity,
Disguised as fortress—worse, immunity—
Is what both parents and their children kill
Each other to possess. Who are we? Hard
To tell. I glimpse my daughter: woman, black,
Pure African (we cannot give her back)
American; she's left her door ajar.

XII. My Daughter's Diary

I'm reading my own innermost debate:
My adolescent daughter's diary.
I read about the need for privacy
And making statements, boys and breaking dates;
I read my agony in passages
About the secret crushes no one knew
I kept, like broken crutches, near the brooms
I used to keep my closet neat. I dredge
Up Jason Wendell—friend, who forced me to
Go down on him. I wondered who to tell
Besides my diary. I was a girl,
I thought. I was humiliated. True
To form, my daughter writes of how she's scared
To talk to me. She doesn't mention why.
I want to change the details. When I cry,
It's all because I can't: invaded, scarred.

XIII. Population Explosion

You mean to say—you've started birth control
And haven't even talked to me? Elise,
This isn't you! I mean you left the case
Right there, on top of all your books. I told
You, and I meant it, that you need to be
Extremely careful what you do these days.
With gonorrhea, syphilis, and AIDS—
And not to even mention pregnancy—
You must be crazy! Having sex is wrong
Until—until you find the one you love.
No daughter raised by me is dumb enough
To risk her life—to risk, yes, everything
We ever worked for, all our hopes and dreams—
You wipe that little smirk of yours right off
Your face. Please, promise me that you'll be safe.
You'll do as I say. See?—you're hurting me.

XIV. The Virgin of Santander

The hands that carved her, holy hands, were men's.
They placed her here, for quiet worshipping.
We do not question her virginity,
As this is not a matter penitents
Need ponder. Take forgiveness from her form,
And pray to her for miracles. This church
Was plundered once by Visigoths; we search
The countryside, through each decaying farm
For relics stolen centuries ago.
And then the French made off with candlesticks
And almost all the gold. But in her box,
The Virgin—isolated, untouched—glows.
We do not question what is miracle.
We have faith. Faith in one God, family.
A faith in what we choose never to see:
What we call relics once were human skulls.

XV. They Break a Lamp Roughhousing

My daughter won't renounce the Protestants;
My son's the little Catholic who states
He'll crucify her. As for me, my faith
Has been reduced to knowing: that I can't
Get married in my parents' church, or take
My children there. A Christian who is gay
Remains enslaved beneath the Bible's grates—
As if times haven't changed since when a steak
Meant excommunication, God meant fear,
And women meant the devil. Read Saint Paul,
Leviticus, my daughter's awful menstrual
Cramps, omens in the slaughtered pig. It's clear
Enlightenment has lost. The meaningless
Still stands to join the victim to the crime.
My daughter sweats until her muscles shine.
I think of Christ, and how she's cursed and blessed.

XVI. The Choice Was Never Made

My daughter must exist before she's raped.
She must exist before I ever live.
(She bears me in her womb. I'll never leave.)
She tells me what to write, and how to say
I want a son, although a daughter is
The part of me my parents didn't want.
I want a son the way my father can't
Pretend he never wanted me: because
We want to love my grandfather, because
My grandfather was unattainable.
Because my father's unavailable,
My daughter must exist in me. She does
Her cartwheels inside my heart for guys
She thinks are cute. She writes her poetry
Inside my ears. She wears like fantasy
My wedding dress. She's happy, and I'm gay.

III

FOR YOU

ALL BEAUTY

For You All Beauty

for Gary Fisher

Because you are so beautiful,
You fall too gracefully; you fall
Because I need to rescue you, until

I lose the meaning of your death.
Try not to focus on the breath
You take before the final cliff—

Imagine the extravagance
Of dying young, your sequined dress
The city lit at night, the dance

So memorable and intimate
That neither partner can forget
How close it felt. Our gazes met—

Fall easily, as beauty ought
To fall. As for your final thought,
Consider what the Romans taught

The people whom they conquered: all
Is beautiful, and what is killed
Returns in monuments. Recall

How beautiful you were; you went
Unyielding to your death, unspent,
Deserving of a monument

Or great cathedral, even Rome
Itself. Imagine, you enthroned
Among those martyrs, you whose crime,

And only crime, was how you loved.
I love you, even as you leave,
So beautiful, so fucking brave

And all emaciated. Touch my face,
My burning cock, my chest. Embrace
Me. Most of all, forgive with grace

Your conquerors, including me.
I fear I loved you greedily.
Or not enough, perhaps, to see

Past monuments, past hospitals—
Just you, alive. I try to tell
Myself you'll live, made beautiful

By AIDS, so beautiful and true,
So unmistakable and true
You'll never die. Remember who

We are. Together, we are more
Than any virus, murderer,
Or monument. The truth—before

You take your final breath, my love—
Is this: beyond this place, above
The clouds, for you all beauty grieves.

The 10,000th AIDS Death
in San Francisco

January 1993

A woman hurried past me in the street
Today, reminding me it's not a dream:
While eating an expensive lunch in some
Expensive Caribbean restaurant
I keep imagining is Cuban-owned,
I notice that I keep imagining
The AIDS ward where I saw a man my age
Die yesterday. I can't say why, but when
He looked at me I wanted him to kiss
My face. I wanted him to live with me
And tell me stories, stories seventeen
Or eighteen hours long, involving sex
Beneath the stars, or with celebrities
Beneath some perfect, countless stars, about
The days before the epidemic killed
So many thousand people. Wanting him
To live, I stood erect beside the bed,
Wanting him. The sex itself was great,
I'm sure, but what I'd really like to know
Was how it felt to know that after lunch
In some expensive restaurant, your friends
Would be alive. Your friends would be alive—
To know no friend would die like that,
Of cryptococcal meningitis, or
Another kind of meningitis, or
A lung infection so severe it makes
A kiss impossible because the need
To breathe is even greater. Hurriedly,
I pay the bill, because I need to breathe
And suddenly I'm seeing stars, I see
Myself outside some Cuban restaurant.
A woman hurries past me, frowning, far.

Safe Sex

Protected in your arms, I dreamed while death
Passed overhead. I guessed I was alive,
Because I heard how faintly in your breath
My name kept being said. We fell in love
When love was not protection in itself;
Misled by poetry, I'd always felt
The pleasures of the tongue were very safe.
Before your urgent pleading face, I knelt
To say your love had come to represent
In me a willingness to die. You came
Inside my mouth, and eagerly death bent
Its ear to listen to my heart. The same
Astonishment without restraint sang out—
Protected in your arms, I died of doubt.

Prescription

We need more drugs. For cancer, with its claws.
For coronary artery disease,
The elephant that sits upon our chests.
For AIDS. For multiple sclerosis too.

We need more drugs, the kinds that obviate
Sharp needles in our veins. The kinds of drugs
Like nitroglycerine beneath our tongues,
The chants of tribal elders, shark fin soups:

We need more drugs for AIDS. The ampules, clear,
Enough for everyone. No side effects.
No clenching quilts until an isolate
Drips out. No blood. For cancer, heart disease;

For multiple sclerosis, AIDS. It's true,
We might make poetry superfluous.
It's true we might become addicted, but
We'd blame ourselves before society,

We'd blame the blood supply, our genes. We'd need
More love, have greed to spare. There'd be no AIDS;
Instead of money, health care bills get paid
In brightly-colored pills that make us dream

This dream: we're insured to the hilt in a world where heart
Disease is curable, where poetry
Was all we ever needed to cure AIDS,
Where victims, all of us, are innocent.

The Good Doctor

A doctor lived in a city
Full of dying men and women.
He ministered to them
A medicine admittedly

Not curative, and only
Slightly toxic. The medicine
Was known as empathy. It worked
Until the doctor grew more lonely—

His patients only died less quickly—
And in a fit of rage
He burned its formula.
Word spread to the sickly

As the virus had: precise
And red, omitting nothing.
The doctor's reputation changed.
No longer was he viewed as wise;

Instead, when patients came
To him they brought suspicion;
They held their breath when he would try
To hear their songs. His names,

Once various and musical,
Were soon forgotten.
When he died of the disease,
They left him where he fell.

TEN PATIENTS, AND ANOTHER

I. Mrs. G.

The patient is a sixty-odd-year-old
White female, who presents with fever, cough,
And shaking chills. No further history
Could be elicited; she doesn't speak.
The patient's social history was non-
Contributory: someone left her here.
The intern on the case heard crackles in
Both lungs. An EKG was done, which showed
A heart was beating in the normal sinus
Rhythm, except for an occasional
Dropped beat. An intravenous line was placed.
The intern found a bruise behind her ear.
She then became quite agitated, and
Began to sob without producing tears.
We think she's dry. She's resting quietly
On Haldol, waiting for a bed upstairs.

II. Jamal

The patient is a three-year-old black male,
The full-term product of a pregnancy
That was, according to his grandmother,
Unplanned and maybe complicated by
Prenatal alcohol exposure. Did
OK, developmentally delayed
But normal weights and heights, until last week
When he ingested what's turned out to be
Cocaine, according to the lab results;
His grandmother had said she'd seen him with
Some baby powder on his face and hands
Before he started seizing and they brought
Him in. The vital signs have stabilized.
The nurse is getting D.S.S. involved.
The mom? She left it on the kitchen table.
That's her—the one who sings to him all night.

III. H.K.

The patient is a twenty-nine-year-old
Black man who lives in Dorchester. Upon
Returning from his shift—the patient is
A night nurse at a local hospital—
He was attacked by two assailants. Males,
White, late teens, shouting threats and epithets.
He thinks they followed him from work. He turned,
Attempting to respond, when he was struck
With two blunt objects in succession. One
Was glass; we know because some fragments were
Extracted from the wounds. He'd bled to a crit
Of twenty, which required stat transfusions.
The surgeons didn't want to operate
Until they had more information. CT scans
Revealed free blood inside the abdomen.
What's scary is he isn't even gay.

IV. Kelly

The patient is a twelve-year-old white female.
She's gravida zero, no STD's.
She'd never even had a pelvic. One
Month nausea and vomiting. No change
In bowel habits. No fever, chills, malaise.
Her school performance has been worsening.
She states that things at home are fine.
On physical exam, she cried but was
Cooperative. Her abdomen was soft,
With normal bowel sounds and question of
A suprapubic mass, which was non-tender.
Her pelvic was remarkable for scars
At six o'clock, no hymen visible,
Some uterine enlargement. Pregnancy
Tests positive times two. She says it was
Her dad. He's sitting in the waiting room.

V. John Doe

An elderly white male, unresponsive.
Looks homeless. Maybe he's been here before:
No chart. No history. His vital signs
Were barely present, temperature was down
Near ninety, pressure ninety over palp;
The pulse was forty, best as they could tell.
They'll hook him to a monitor before
They warm him up. I didn't listen to
His lungs—I bet I'd hear a symphony
In there. I couldn't check his pupils since
His lids were frozen shut, but there were no
External signs of trauma to the head.
They found this picture of a woman with
Two tiny kids still pinned inside his coat.
It's only three A.M. The night's young. If
He's lucky, by tomorrow he'll be dead.

VI. S.W.

Extending from her left ear down her jaw,
The lac was seven centimeters long.
She told me that she slipped and struck her face
Against the kitchen floor. The floor was wet
Because she had been mopping it. I guessed
She'd had to wait for many hours since
The clock read nearly midnight; who mops floors
So late? Her little girl kept screaming in
Her husband's thick, impatient arms: he knocked
Three times, each time to ask when we'd be done.
I infiltrated first with lidocaine.
She barely winced, and didn't start to cry
Until the sixteenth stitch went in and we
Were almost through. I thought my handiwork
Was admirable. I yawned, then offered her
Instructions on the care of wounds. She left.

VII. Manuel

In Trauma 1, a gay Latino kid—
I think he's seventeen—is getting tubed
For respiratory failure. "Sleeping pills
And Tylenol," I translated for him
As he was wheeled in. His *novio*
Explained that when he'd told his folks about
It all, they threw him out. Like trash. They lived
Together underneath the overpass
Of Highway 101 for seven weeks,
The stars obstructed from their view. For cash,
They sucked off older men in Cadillacs;
A *viejita* from the neighborhood
Brought *tacos* to them secretly. Last night,
With eighteen-wheelers roaring overhead,
He whispered that he'd lost the will to live.
He pawned his crucifix to get the pills.

VIII. F.P.

Another AIDS admission. This one's great:
They bring him in strapped down because he threw
His own infected shit at them—you better bring
Your goggles!—and a mask, we think he's got
TB. He's pissed as hell. Apparently,
He wants to die at home but somebody
Keeps calling 911. A relative
Back home in Iowa, or some damn place.
Just keep him snowed with Ativan—believe
You me, you do not want to get to know
This fucker. Kaposi's all over, stinks
Like shit—incontinent, of course. How long
Before you get down here? Because his nurse
Is driving me insane. Of course we got
Blood cultures . . . yeah, a gas—OK, I'll stick
Him one more time. The things you do for love.

IX. Tommy

A twenty-one-year-old white man brought in
By ambulance—in hypotensive shock,
Shot in the back while buying drugs from three
Black men. The cord must be involved:
His legs are paralyzed, his penis is
Erect, and all sensation from below
The level of the entry site is lost.
They left him in the street for dead; I heard
Them say an alley dog was lapping up
His blood like milk when he was found. Before
He goes to surgery, he has to give
Informed consent, which he's refused to do
Thus far. He states he'd rather die than be
Dependent on his family for care.
They're questioning his competence, of course.
They're waiting on his folks. His wife just stares.

X. Maria

This G2, P1 gives us a confusing
History. It sounds like she's been pregnant
Approximately thirty weeks, although
She can't recall her LMP. No pain,
But bleeding for about two days. Of course
She hasn't had prenatal care, and God
Only knows where the father is. She works
Two jobs that keep her on her feet all day.
She's been in the United States six months,
And doesn't speak a word of English. Bet
You she's illegal. Cervical exam
Is unremarkable, the os is closed.
I think we need an ultrasound to tell
Us more. Besides a look at the placenta,
We need some confirmation of her dates.
Her uterus can tell us more than she can.

XI. Jane Doe #2

They found her unresponsive in the street
Beneath a lamplight I imagined made
Her seem angelic, regal even, clean.
She must have been around sixteen. She died
Who knows how many hours earlier
That day, the heroin inside her like
A vengeful dream about to be fulfilled.
Her hands were crossed about her chest, as though
Raised up in self-defense; I tried to pry
Them open to confirm the absence of
A heartbeat, but in death she was so strong,
As resolute as she was beautiful.
I traced the track marks on her arms instead,
Then pressed my thumb against her bloodless lips,
So urgent was my need to know. I felt
The quiet left by a departing soul.

Confession

The neuroradiologist in me
Is looking over scans impatiently.
So many imperfections, brains in ink.
By simply looking at them, one might think

Them harmless slugs, both unoriginal
And clearly thoughtless: what's become of all
The energy we had? The joy of sex?
A culture is the billboards it erects,

Some smart-ass sociologist has said,
Or probably has said. Yet in these heads
There must be more than squishy pinkish stuff,
A lust for learning maybe, space enough

For all the people in a shrinking world,
For all the children orphaned in the war
That's never-ending. If I grieve for us,
Forgive me for my airs. It's obvious

That I'm in love, or very recently
Was burglarized. But what you'll never see,
My Little Turtle Dove, my Squeaky Squeak,
Is in the heart. My brain was always weak;

I've tried to find the lesion, but I can't.
Before a senseless trial, I'll recant
And go to prison anyway. My heart
Will break all promises, and it will hurt.

Lost in the Hospital

It's not that I don't like the hospital.
Those small bouquets of flowers, pert and brave.
The smell of antiseptic cleansers.
The ill, so wistful in their rooms, so true.
My friend, the one who's dying, took me out
To where the patients go to smoke, IV's
And oxygen in tanks attached to them—
A tiny patio for skeletons. We shared
A cigarette, which was delicious but
Too brief. I held his hand; it felt
Like someone's keys. How beautiful it was,
The sunlight pointing down at us, as if
We were important, full of life, unbound.
I wandered for a moment where his ribs
Had made a space for me, and there, beside
The thundering waterfall of his heart,
I rubbed my eyes and thought, "I'm lost."

IV

CANCIONES

DE LA

MUERTE

SONG BEFORE DYING

for Marilyn Hacker

I. A Diagnostic Procedure Was Performed

I have a cancer in my arm. I write
So I can see it better—on the page—
The words traversing the malignant stage
Of countless, hungry cells as they divide
Until I'm drained of something horrible.
It's not the cancer, but the thoughts I fear.
I recognize it came from me. I hear
The pitter-patter of the pseudopods,
I hear my parents whispering. (My arm
Is like a microphone.) The center of
My face, it seems a place I never loved—
I have a cancer. Growing fast as germs.
It looks so harmless when it's poetry.
It looks so delicate, this shaking pen,
This cursive script I learned when I was ten—
The cancer in my arm is killing me.

II. The Accident

I broke the bone while I was flying down
A hill on skis. I hardly even fell.
The ski patrol arrived—they heard me yell,
I guess—although I don't recall the sound,
I thought I'd seen an angel, or a hawk
Descend upon a kill. The pain was screws;
The mountains, one gigantic fist punched through
The earth. The youngest said, "I think it's broke—
Hey dude, you broke your arm—cool!" Nervously,
Another struggled with the cloth cravat.
Another, hand outstretched: I'd lost my hat,
And he would give me his. He grinned at me,
And something in his teeth and kindness said,
Ominously, I would remember him.
I wonder whether I was saved. Back home,
This cast upon my arm, I wish I'd died.

III. Phone Call

"I'm looking at your X-rays here. How old
Are you again? That's right, you're twenty-six.
And you've had surgery, you say, to fix
The nerve? I see. And does your hand get cold?
OK, good. Any other symptoms? Pain?
Excellent. Well, I'd like you to come in.
To get a CAT scan of your arm. There's been
Some changes in the bone around—a change,
Yes, nothing serious I hope—around
The fracture site. Now normally, these cysts
Just go away. But yours is getting worse.
I don't want you to worry—just come down
And let us have a closer look. Today.
This afternoon if possible. Yes, yes—
I want to move aggressively on this.
Good. Now, you're *sure* you haven't had some pain?"

IV. Love

It's not enough—to tell you this, as if
You didn't know exactly what bad shape
My heart is in: they've chopped it out and placed
It on our shelf, to watch while it rolls off.
I love you, though it isn't cruel enough
To watch you breakfasting alone and think
It's not much different to walk the brink
Of life alone. Because, although you love
Me, nothing you can do can bring me back.
There's not enough of love in the entire
Begotten world for that. So toss my lyre
Into the flames, with me. And as the black
Crawls over us, remember what we said
At breakfast, how we said we couldn't love
Each other quite enough; that I might live
Again to touch your lips, raised from the dead.

V. I Dream a Cure

I think these painkillers are altering
My mental state too much. Just yesterday,
I woke believing that I'd never die.
I dreamt that I was Martin Luther King;
A sea of pain and desperation stretched
Before me while I gave my speech. Police
Were beating protesters. A girl in lace
Exploded, arms akimbo, as we watched
A bomb go off inside a church. I begged
For mercy, pleaded with the crowd for peace,
Explained away, in tears, indignities.
And as they bound me, I was calm—my legs
Thick lead behind the podium, the shot
And sudden bullet with its metal arms
Enclosing me until my breath was gone,
Until an armless girl untied my knots.

VI. The Next Poem Could Be Your Last

Imagine death. No fun. No poetry.
No further arguments with relatives.
No work to do. No boring life to live.
Imagine, death: like making pottery
Or writing eulogies, it takes some skill
To do it passably. Like argument,
It needs resistance to be shaped against.
Like relatives you fight the urge to kill,
You know you won't. Like work, there's never less
Of it. Imagine: death is almost life.
Except it's fascinating, like a knife.
You lose yourself just staring at the edge.
You lose yourself and suddenly you're not
Alive, you're dying and for fun you try
To write your eulogy. You tell some lies,
Pretend you're wry and brave. Imagine that.

VII. Aunt Mary

My father shook me gently. When I woke,
My room was dark, and as he said she'd died
I thought we were inside her coffin—dead,
With her. My father cried all through the wake,
And someone shook me gently while he said,
"She loved you very much." And when I saw
The coffin lid was sealed shut (because
Her wounds were so disfiguring) I bled
All through the roses—roses, red and rich,
The inner petals pulsing, shivering,
As in her womb, the baby struggling
To free itself. They'd found her in a ditch,
I overheard them saying, fifty feet
From where the cars had crashed—my mother's hands
Shaking gently, trying to understand
How no one knew about her pregnancy.

VIII. The Will to Die

I listen to Respighi, eyes half-closed;
I know my internship begins in June.
I listen carefully, my ears attuned
To each exquisite note the piccolo
Produces, sharp, like light that penetrates
Venetian blinds. I know my internship
Begins in June. I'd love to make that trip
To Italy. See the gondolas. Pompeii,
Those figures made of ash. I know about
Responsibility, the work I love;
I know that they're expecting me to live.
But "No!" is what the rising music shouts,
The violins my heart, the cello deep
Inside my bones, the ancient dances, airs—
The music grows from me, gives back my hair—
I think of Italy, and fall asleep.

IX. The Very Self

Another end-stage cancer patient came
For hospice placement yesterday. It seemed
As though he'd lived forever in the same
Misshapen body, starving for a name
To give each new-found bone. It seemed as though
He'd run until his muscles were consumed,
Until his gnawing hunger had subsumed
In it his very self. I need to know
His vital signs. I want to know his fate.
I need to hold his heart, the stone beneath
The endless, bone-strewn desert; while I squeeze
For just one drop of blood, more dying waits
Downstairs for me. I almost hear their groans.
Same hunger, bones. Same face we all consumed.
As I examine them, I find the tomb
Toward which they lead. I know it is my own.

X. Life Is Sacred

I'm writing this so no one tries to ram
A plastic tube straight down my trachea;
As for my organs, you may take them all.
You healthy people ought to give a damn
About a dying person's last requests.
I can't control my cancer; no one can,
Despite seductive faiths the healers chant.
You must respect my right to say what's best
For me, to judge my quality of life
Myself. Religion long ago expelled
Me from its dull-eyed flock; I won't be told
My life is sacred. Spend the money left
In my insurance saving children from
Leukemia, or finding cures for what
I have. I'm far too pissed—and sane—to rot
Inside a hospital until my freedom comes.

XI. My Favorite Season

Come, harvest me before the winter stills
My heart, definitive and matter-of-fact
As ice. To die with all my hues intact,
To burn with apples in my hands until
I smell my sweetness in the air—it's true,
There is a strange redemption in the harvest
And if October's anything, it's vengeance,
Betrayal, lust for life. The sky is blue,
As only red and orange in the earth
Can make it blue; the earth is dying but
It doesn't seem to care—it celebrates
Its death. Come, harvest me until your hearth
Is gorged with flames and roasting meats, until
The air begins to smell this sweet—before
The winter comes, its claws and scores
Of fangs and icicles, all bared to kill.

XII. The Patient-Doctor Relationship

I feared they would refuse to operate,
Or test my blood without informed consent.
I've never been among the militant
On either side of this oft-heard debate:
The patient has the right to privacy,
And more importantly, the right to care;
The doctor has a need to know, it's fair
To say, the patient's risk of HIV
Infection. Somewhere in between, we lose
Our heads. Insurance companies, should they
Find out, might terminate your policy;
You find your doctor's office door slammed closed.
Suppose: a doctor who is gay becomes
A patient. Cancer in a bone, let's say.
He tells, and soon the word is spreading. Days
Go by; they never call. My plight begins.

XIII. Amputee

What rotten luck: a slot machine that's jinxed,
A one-armed bandit emptying itself
Of coins, its self-esteem. I see myself,
Or what is left of me, and when I think
Of what it's like to have one arm, how pure
I'll be, how asymmetrical and odd,
I want another chance to spin, ask God
For better luck, or better, for a cure—
I raise my arm, then jerk it down and wish
For watermelons, lemons, dollar signs,
My brain is spinning now, I've lost my mind,
I'm gambling with everything I miss—
My normal life, his kiss, the awful arm
That wanders through the night in search of me.
I want to lose it all, thunderously,
The gold coins swollen rivers in the storm.

XIV. Just the Facts

Pathology report: received, en bloc,
A specimen that's labeled ARM, RIGHT
Belonging to a patient Campo. Weight
Ten kilograms. The specimen is pink.
It measures sixty centimeters long,
Eight wide, and fourteen in circumference.
The surgeon's case report in conference
Today described—correct me if I'm wrong—
A twenty-six year old, still healthy, with
A history of minor trauma to
The right arm, skiing accident, and who
Presented for routine exam some months
Ago—his CAT scan demonstrating changes
Within the cortex of the healing bone
Consistent with malignancy. He's come
To surgery. They want to know his chances.

XV. Lilacs for My Mother

Of all the drugs I've known, the lilac's sweetest.
I seek it in the gardens of my neighbors;
To walk intoxicated through its vapors,
I've visited the Arnold Arboretum
(Which has the largest plants—a century
Of cultivation, blooming, on display).
The scent recalls my mother's silk sachets . . .
I'm resting on her pillow. In the breeze,
She sings to me: she says I'm handsome, strong;
I'm all she ever dreamed of, perfect, loved.
It never mattered that I'm gay; above
All else (the breeze, remembering her song)
Is freedom to express our love, be who
We are. And so, about my arm? It doesn't matter.
The lilacs, through my tears, grow even fatter—
My mother is my heart. The lilacs bloom.

XVI. Resurrection

They called just now to say the surgery
Is off. Like that, without explaining why.
I wrap my arms around myself, and cry.
My body still seems alien to me,
At first; but as the afternoon grows vast
And patterned on my bedroom wall, across
The pictures of me hugging friends, my loss
Seems almost silly, and my heart beats fast—
I'm rowing us across a river, fresh
And muscular. I know the river's name,
But keep forgetting it. He looks the same,
That smile, brilliant as silver fish;
I know that place upon a hill we go
To picnic, then make love. The river's black.
I want so much to speak, but can't look back.
That sound—the phone's been ringing—them! "Hello?"

THE IMMORTAL SONG

for Mary B. Campbell

I. Rebirth

Inventing panaceas late last night,
I stumbled on a formula for life.
I mixed a wine glass with a paring knife,
And ended up with blood. My blood was quite
Remarkable, and red, so red it turned
The water in the bathtub red. I knew
What I was giving up, but tell me, who
Could choose mere comfort over the return
To blissful, everlasting peace? The sphere
That I inhabit now is full of us.
We're angels, infants, stars. We're numinous,
And hate the weight of words. We may appear
To you, as *déjà vu* among the frozen foods,
Or on the highway in the form of deer
You almost kill before your speeding car—
There is eternal life. Damn, is it good.

II. The Doctor

Essential hypertension, uncontrolled,
Is almost immortality. The pressure
Of blood inside the arteries I measure
With mercury, reflecting on the soul:
Both liquid and a heavy metal, trapped
And beautiful—a subtle trembling—cold.
I hate to watch my patients growing old.
I watch as blood pressures ascend, hearts stop;
A cancer dimpling a woman's breast,
As if to pull her in, inside herself.
On certain days, I want to die myself,
Then live forever by a perfect test:
My blood shows infinite cholesterol
And nothing cures me of my needs, and I've
Among my bitter medicines no salve
To calm my troubled, trembling soul.

III. Superman Is Dead

I used to think that immortality
Was just like Superman, without the tights
And cape—just flying naked through the sky,
As muscled as the clouds, able to leap
Tall buildings in a single bound. I thought
To be invincible was what it meant—
To live forever! I was innocent.
Back then, I hadn't learned the words they taught,
Like hemochromatosis, kryptonite.
And now, I wonder whether words do weigh
Upon the soul. I wonder if I say
Your name urgently enough at night,
Might you descend and hold me in your arms
Again, like Superman but naked, free
And muscled as the clouds, able to leap
Back into bed, your body hard and warm.

IV. The Rain Forest

In Venezuela, forests still exist
Whose age is measured in millennia.
A universe unto themselves, beyond
The reach of human hands that would exhaust
Their varied resources, they contemplate
The future of the planet. Oxygen
Is how they argue, translating the sun
Into a language so articulate,
So true, that all can understand the thrust
Of what they say. When I was young, I sat
Beneath their canopy of voices, wet
With dew. I couldn't hear the cities rust
At all, because my heart was filled with words.
I wish I could remember what they said.
It wasn't agony, but it was sad
As shrinking streams, the vanishing of birds.

V. Prayer

My father, who's in heaven, hollered out
My name. His kingdom came, his will was done,
On earth that was just like heaven. "God damn,"
I thought I heard him say, "we must dole out
The daily bread." Give me this day, I thought.
Give me this one day to live, really live.
I can't escape my trespasses—forgive
Me, father, my trespasses—see, I brought
The bread. Hey, are you even listening?
I said, forgive us our trespasses
As we forgive those sinners who trespass
Against us. Our father, hear me sing.
Because I sing about redemption, man's
Utter fallibility. Lead us not
Into temptation—see, Father, I am not
Evil, not immortal. Deliver me. Amen.

VI. DNA, or, The Legend of My Grandfather

A molecule that craves its own embrace
Encodes a message from my ancestors:
Survival means eternal life. Restored
As though he were alive again, my face
Seems more my grandfather's than mine. I search
The contours of my jaws for what he'd say—
In tissue overlying bone, nucle-
Ic acids fast unzipped to base-pairs (matched
In stews primordial) give rise to cells,
Retell their ageless story. Cartilage
Is synthesized; I have no heritage
Except the mitochondria which mill
About my cytoplasm, full of sparks—
I am consumed by my autolysins
Yet constantly rebuilt by selfish genes,
Become my grandfather who killed a shark.

VII. The Ceiling

Beneath a handprint on a stucco ceiling,
I fucked another man. It was my first
Time making love. It all happened so fast
I didn't even know what I was feeling.
I didn't even realize that time
Was passing; each sweep of the ceiling fan
Lopped moments from my life. A stranger's hand
Had left its mark, and made an urgent mime—
An ageless presence—from the white-faced room.
The silent warning told me don't go on,
Or beckoned me to pleasures found beyond
This life. I looked to where his hard-on loomed
At me, and laid my hand across his chest.
Somehow, I felt saved. Later on, I read
The Bible while he shaved, and understood:
Against the falling heavens, I had pressed.

VIII. Homage to Shakespeare

A friend of mine explained to me how she
Once used a volume of your work to kill
An ant that crawled across her window sill.
She missed your point on immortality,
I guess. My brother read your sonnets, stoned
Beyond belief on pot he smoked in a skull-
Shaped bong—to him, it was a miracle
That anyone, alive or dead, could hone
A song to so precise a note. I guess
He understood the workings of your ear.
A famous critic of your verse says here
That you thought love was an unwillingness
To die, and that the pen could somehow stave
Off time. So who am I to write like this,
To offer you, cross centuries, my kiss—
The ant, the skull, the one who can't be saved?

IX. Your Voice

Last night, when we made love, I saw inside
Your voice, how cavernous it was, and full of wings.
I wandered through it, not quite suffering
But drenched in sweat. Your mouth was magnified,
As was my heart, beyond the size of God,
Beyond the vast red size an open rose
Can grow when held beneath the love-struck nose—
So this is immortality, I said,
With skin and sweat instead of words; my mouth
Was full of you, your voice, your ears, your thighs.
I saw inside your eyes, and mystified
By them, I asked you questions about death.
You answered me with moans, and in your semen
I tasted life, I tasted rain, and then
I brushed my thumb across your dimpled chin
Since you were smiling, rose-voiced, sent from heaven.

X. No. 160

The poetry of Michelangelo
Is said to pale in comparison
To his accomplishment in paint and stone.
I saw his *David* many years ago,
In junior high. It made me want to kill
Myself. I'm not sure why, except it seemed
So final in its beauty, so consumed
By its demand to live. I lacked the will
Back then; instead, I wrote a poem that rhymed
About a kid whose empty heart contained
Some lies about a girlfriend, told in vain.
Tonight I read his *Rima*, in bed in Rome:
What I remember now is David's face
Without the body, in a sonnet that is not
A painting but is words, a sculpture that
Is made from silk, saying *raise me from this place.*

XI. Lunatic Fringe

I'm dying for the millionth time, my ship
Disintegrating in a million bits.
My enemies, the evil Lunatics,
Are even more immortal: blip by blip
They swarm, until the universe becomes
This frenzied, hot pursuit. I kill them by
The dozens but they won't relent. I die
Again, by bombs, my buzzing laser guns
Against the backdrop of the stars a last
Weak brilliance, like the parting of a soul.
But then, reanimated, in control,
I'm cruising through those galaxies I'd lost,
I kill them with my buzzing laser guns,
Pursuing them because they are alive,
Because I'm drunk on all my million lives,
More bonus points—an asteroid—I'm done!

XII. Money and God

The economic indicators say
There's money to be made in saving souls.
That banks that lend to churches don't foreclose:
They know the Lord provides, and flocks will pay.
What would God say of all the innocence
Republicans and moneylenders stole?
There's money to be made in saving souls,
Alright. The price of broken promises
Is cheap as immortality. It costs
The faithful grandmother of three
The money she'd have spent to fix her knee,
While toes of televangelists are washed
By prostitutes in new Jacuzzis. Sure,
There's money to be made in saving souls.
We've only these; what else have we to sell?
I pray that through the greed we can endure.

XIII. Ode to a Nightingale

Madonna, you're immortal. You're so hot,
You make the sunlight seem like ice inside
Those diamonds that you flaunt. I almost died,
That time I saw your concert, and it hurt
So much when I jerked off the fourth time—damn,
I wanted you, I wanted just to be
Like you, your tits and muscles pressing me
Down low, your voice ethereal-like, dim—
The dawn outside, everywhere, reaching in
To touch us on the bed, the strawberries
I feed you tasting like sweet poetry,
The dawn forgiving us, long fingers, thin,
Until it's saying something in the silver dish
About what yearning is—damn, you're so fine
Madonna, you're like the most expensive wine
In the world being gone, leaving just a wish.

XIV. Antidote

The virus replicates inside the cell.
The virus cannot live without its host.
The virus hides. The virus kills its host,
But not before it spreads into the cells
Of someone else, another host. It kills
That which it needs to live. It hides
Inside a cell. I have no place to hide:
I'm the host the virus wants to kill.
You see, the killing virus has no soul.
The virus cannot live without my life.
The virus replicates. It needs my life
To live, but it can never have my soul.
The soulless, killing virus replicates
Inside my cells. I am its host. I die
By cells each day. I know, the more I die,
It's me the virus never replicates.

XV. The Terrible Percussion of the Host

The vessel in his brain had burst; inside
His skull, a rose of blood was blooming, hot
And full. Inside his head, his beating heart
Unfolded like a dream that he had died
A death like this before, that he had bled
From merely thinking about roses, thorns
And fragrance like the smell of being born—
He was ascending toward the light ahead,
The light an oxygen unbreathable
Except by souls, the light a form of hope
Itself, and as he died he did not grope
For meaning, light exploding in his skull
Until the light was everything and he
Was weightless and alive again as though
He'd been forgiven, or possessed, by those
Proclaiming loudly immortality.

XVI. The View from Here

The view from here is breathtaking; the air
Is stratospheric, absolutely clear.
It's nearly operatic, what I hear
When sunlight strikes the headlands, hillsides bared
By drought across the bay. I wonder what
It's like, to be so timelessly extant,
To have been formed by processes one can't
Imagine—shakings of the earth, the weight
Of polar icecaps, lava boiling in the sea—
The faintest outlines of creation, here.
The wind begins to rearrange my hair,
Reminds me of my presence. Willfully,
I write this down, trying to record
The truth. "The view from here is breathtaking."
I pause, and hold my breath until I sing
This opus, made entirely of words.

V

WHAT THE

BODY TOLD

My Childhood in Another
Part of the World

The world was quiet then.
A child was playing dead,
Avoiding being immunized.
I lived in Venezuela when

Democracies could kill.
A child was turning red,
Beneath a sun he understood
Was angry. Miracle

Of miracles, the world
Was children taking guns
Away from soldiers—run!
Through streets like mental wards.

The world confused me then.
A child was clenching in
His fist the Ritalin
He would not take. In mine,

I shielded a secret thing:
A large, bright-emerald beetle.
Revealed, it would startle
Adults, who thought it menacing.

My childhood, my childhood,
Return to me. I was
Too dumb to be unwise,
Too young to be so unafraid.

What We All Want

The selfishness of what I do
Is clear. I read, as if the truth
Weren't evident, as if the proof

Of my humanity were more
A novel than what I've endured
Myself each day: caricatured

(My own reflection in the glass
Is anyone but me), harassed
(The pimply teenager in class

Who asks, "What use is poetry?"),
Demoralized. It's plain to see
The point of what I do is me—

To make from heavy cloudy days
Huge, gently lowered silver trays,
To make from bubble-baths champagne,

To render my experience,
However poor, magnificent.
It takes imagination. Let's pretend:

We write to glorify the self,
We read to fill the empty shelves,
We listen, wistfully, to shells

And sometimes hear the ocean roar.
Today, I saw an open door
And worried I might drown, like scores

Of others with my illness. Once
I thought I might succeed. But when
I lost it all—my stocks and bonds,

My clothes, my swollen shelves—I knew.
I wasn't selfish, or a brute.
Just naked, human. I was you.

The Cuban Sky

Remembering is just another form,
Or so it seems from here, of distance. I
Remember farms, alfalfa growing dry—
It could be Spain or California, warm
Light spilled rum on a terra-cotta floor.
It's far away, it's centuries ago,
Before my father made the journey he
Would not retrace. It's odd, because I read
The poetry of Michelangelo
As if he wrote it only yesterday,
For me. Remembering is hard for me.
So much, so far away—the history
Of the rebellion, empty victories—
My father, through the bullets, heard the sea.
It could be Spain or California, France
Or Italy. I see the farm. We grow
The sugar cane we turn to rum. It's dry—
A bowl of black figs on the sill, a knife,
The poetry of Michelangelo
Is what my parents read to me. It's dry,
The sugar cane—it seems my knife is dull—
Or is it fields of alfalfa, or the sky
Before remembering the Cuban sky
Was, despite my father's love, not possible?

Madrid

A glimpse of her. Dark sunglasses, her mouth
A man's wounds, her black hair rising in the wind.
Her black hair, flag of death, a Muslim prayer.
A shadow trying to absorb the sun.
Her black hair, Spanish everywhere, her dress
A river swelled with blood, her black hair bulls
Charging through the streets, her black hair crows and crows,
The centuries of crows, the Spanish sun
Eclipsed. Red dress, red lipstick drawn like blood.
Her black hair everywhere, unending, black.
The wind and Spanish everywhere, the blood,
Her mouth a story in her blood. Her hair,
The sun. I see Madrid, so beautiful.

In English That Is Spanish

You'd never understand why I'm confused.
I'd give you explanations if I could:
I'd write in Spanish just this once except
My pen keeps making English from my thoughts.
I'd write from deserts, or from jungles, but
It's autumn and I can't ignore these flames—
I can't ignore the fact I'm not in Spain—
But one's surroundings aren't languages.
(I still wish for a rainy season, but my droughts
Go on and on.) I wish I'd been
In Spain just once, to watch the Englishmen
Wash up on shore, I wish I'd heard them learn
The Spanish of my ancestors. I'd write
In perfect English if I could. I'd write
A sonnet just like Lorca, I'd write *El Cid*;
My English would be Spanish-sounding, rhyme
Would be so effortless I'd make you cry.
I'd make you cry in languages begun
Before there were two countries in the world,
In languages you'd want to make exist,
So one grand poetry sufficed. I'd write
To you in English and in Spanish, and
You'd understand that immortality
Is really only going back in time
Through languages like fourth dimensions, rhymes
Like clocks, to when we were a single race,
A single human being crying out
For rain, or fire from the falling leaves,
With no one ready to misunderstand.

My Voice

To cure myself of wanting Cuban songs,
I wrote a Cuban song about the need
For people to suppress their fantasies,
Especially unhealthy ones. The song
Began by making reference to the sea,
Because the sea is like a need so great
And deep it never can be swallowed. Then
The song explores some common myths
About the Cuban people and their folklore:
The story of a little Carib boy
Mistakenly abandoned to the sea;
The legend of a bird who wanted song
So desperately he gave up flight; a queen
Whose strength was greater than a rival king's.
The song goes on about morality,
And then there is a line about the sea,
How deep it is, how many creatures need
Its nourishment, how beautiful it is
To need. The song is ending now, because
I cannot bear to hear it any longer.
I call this song of needful love my voice.

Remembering Why

Whatever has been said before, forget
It now. Forget the words you knew until
Today, because today I will invent
Another form of what you might have said.
It's like debriefing. Let's begin: I knew

A language once upon a time so strange
I was unable to express my thoughts
With it. The language had a name, like Sense
Or Urge or something similar to that.
It seemed so beautiful, so distant, so

Unspeakable I was afraid of it.
I was afraid of my own mouth, of what
It might contain. And in my fear I found
What seemed a passageway at first, which then
Became a way I could communicate

With other people like myself. (Before
You think me patently insane, allow
Me to explain; like languages, the mind
Is many-faceted and sometimes hard
To reconstruct.) I listened, and I heard

A sound that was familiar, murmuring
Like water running in a hidden stream.
I searched for it, which somehow made me sing.
The search itself was song; it was inside
My lungs that I was lost. I recognize

Some elements of this sad history
Are true for all of us. Why else would we
Read poetry? The space that I now know
Must be inside of you exists in me
As well. We are connected by a song,

A river, caverns, fears. Another way
Of saying we have language, I suppose.
The world we see is simply what one knows

About himself. Outside, the chasm grows
While on this couch I have begun to doze

And in my dream I watch you with one eye,
Which speaks to you like language does, in lies.
In corners of the room, two babies cry.
We search for them, we know they soon shall die
While helpless we are searching, knowing why.

El Día de los Muertos

In Mexico, I met myself one day
Along the side of someone's private road.
I recognized the longing in my face,
I felt the heavy burden of the load
I carried. Mexico, I thought, was strange
And very dry. The private road belonged
To friends more powerful than I, enraged
But noble people who like me sang songs
In honor of the dead. In Mexico,
Tradition is as heavy as the sun.
I stared into my eyes. Some years ago,
I told myself, I met a handsome man
Who thought that I was Mexican. The weight
Of some enormous pain, unspeakable
Yet plain, was in his eyes; his shirt was white,
So white it blinded me. After it all
Became more clear, and we were making love
Beneath the cool sheet of the moon, I knew
We were alive. The tiny stars above
Seemed strange and very far. A dry wind blew.
I gave myself to him, and then I asked
Respectfully if I might touch his face.
I did not want to die. His love unmasked,
I saw that I had slept not with disgrace
But with desire. Along the desert road,
A cactus bloomed. As water filled my eyes,
I sang a song in honor of the dead.
They came for me. My grief was like a vise,
And in my blood I felt the virus teem.
My noble friends abandoned me beside
The road. The sun, awakened from its dream,
Rose suddenly. I watched it as I died,
And felt the heaviness of all its gold.
I listened for the singing in the distance.
A man walked toward me. The story he told
Seemed so familiar, pained, and so insistent,

I wished I would live long enough to hear
Its end. This man was very kind to me.
He kissed me, gave me water, held me near.
In Mexico, they sing exquisitely.

Safe Sex Revisited

In retrospect, I knew I was in love—
And what is love without the risk of some
Catastrophe to be someday relived?
Returning to what otherwise might seem
The moment of my greatest joy, I've learned
A power to protect myself from AIDS.
I call it "Poetry of the Absurd."
I give myself to him; this time, I'm wearing shades
And I'm unknowable. The virus tries
To penetrate, but I write poetry
And so it finds no place to multiply—
My blood cells are replaced by words for "bleed,"
My penis is a pen with which I write
These contradictions. Everywhere is night.

What the Body Told

Not long ago, I studied medicine.
It was terrible, what the body told.
I'd look inside another person's mouth,
And see the desolation of the world.
I'd see his genitals and think of sin.

Because my body speaks the stranger's language,
I've never understood those nods and stares.
My parents held me in their arms, and still
I think I've disappointed them; they care
And stare, they nod, they make their pilgrimage

To somewhere distant in my heart, they cry.
I look inside their other-person's mouths
And see the sleek interior of souls.
It's warm and red in there—like love, with teeth.
I've studied medicine until I cried

All night. Through certain books, a truth unfolds.
Anatomy and physiology,
The tiny sensing organs of the tongue—
Each nameless cell contributing its needs.
It was fabulous, what the body told.

Rafael Campo is a practicing physician at Harvard Medical School and
the Beth Israel Hospital in Boston. He is the author of *The Other Man
Was Me: A Voyage to the New World*, a selection in the National Poetry
Series 1993 Open Competition. Campo's poems have appeared in *The
Kenyon Review, The Threepenny Review, The Nation, Ploughshares, Best
American Poetry 1995*, and other publications.

Library of Congress Cataloging-in-Publication Data
Campo, Rafael.
What the body told / Rafael Campo.
ISBN 0-8223-1733-8 (cl: alk. paper). —ISBN 0-8223-1742-7 (pb: alk. paper)
I. Title. PS3553.A4883W48 1996
811'.54—dc20   95-36519 CIP